Little Skill Seekers

WORD FAMILIES

SCHOLASTIC

New York • Toronto • London • Auckland • Sydney • New Delhi
Mexico City • Hong Kong • Buenos Aires

Cover Design: Tannaz Fassihi
Cover Illustration: Michael Robertson
Interior Design: Mina Chen
Interior Illustration: Doug Jones

Scholastic Inc., 557 Broadway, New York, NY 10012
ISBN: 978-1-338-30639-2
First printing, March 2019.

1 2 3 4 5 6 7 8 9 10   40   24 23 22 21 20 19

Dear Parent,

Welcome to *Little Skill Seekers: Word Families*! Recognizing common sound-spelling patterns increases a child's ability to read, spell, and decode unfamiliar words—this workbook will help your child develop these skills.

Help your little skill seeker build a strong foundation for learning by choosing more books in the Little Skill Seekers series. The exciting and colorful workbooks in the series are designed to set your child on the path to success. Each book targets essential skills important to your child's development.

Here are some key features of *Little Skill Seekers: Word Families* and the other workbooks in this series:

- Filled with colorful illustrations that make learning fun and playful

- Provides plenty of opportunity to practice essential skills

- Builds independence as children work through the pages on their own, at their own pace

- Comes in a perfect size that fits easily in a backpack for practice on the go

Now let's get started on this journey to help your child become a successful, lifelong learner!

—The Editors

Write -am to finish each word.

 c|

 h

 j

 y

Make more -am words. Use the word wheel. Write the words. We did the first one for you.

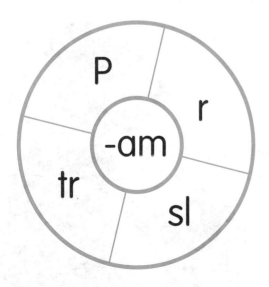

1. _____ram_____

2. _____

3. _____

4. _____

Write -an to finish each word.

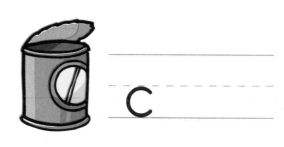 c _____

 m _____

 f _____

 v _____

Make more -an words. Use the word wheel. Write the words. We did the first one for you.

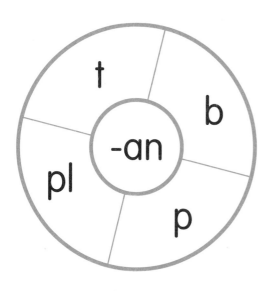

1. _____ ban _____

2. _____

3. _____

4. _____

Write -ap to finish each word.

c|_____ c_____

m_____ n_____

Make more -ap words. Use the word wheel. Write the words. The first one is done for you.

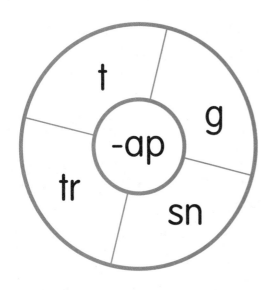

1. _____ gap _____

2. _____

3. _____

4. _____

Write -at to finish each word.

**Make more -at words. Use the word wheel. Write the words.
The first one is done for you.**

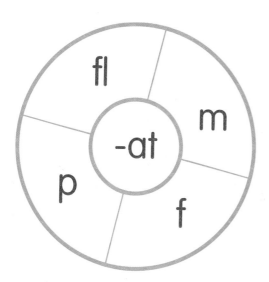

1. _____ mat _____

2. _____

3. _____

4. _____

Use the Letter Bank to complete the words in each row.

Letter Bank			
h r tr	_____am	_____am	_____am
c r v	_____an	_____an	_____an
m c fl	_____ap	_____ap	_____ap
b r s	_____at	_____at	_____at

Sort the words below into word families.
Write each word in the chart where it belongs.

swam
ran
snap
fan
pan
pat
am
dam
yam
sap
chat

map	cat	van	clam
1			
2			
3			
4			

How many of each did you find? Write the number below.

-ap _____   -at _____   -an _____   -am _____

Which word family has the most words? _____

Add the letters in each box to make words in that word family. Write each word.

-am

h + am = _____

cl + am = _____

-ap

m + ap = _____

n + ap = _____

Use an -am or -ap word from above to finish each sentence. The first one is done for you.

Dan took a _____nap_____ on the sofa.

Kam found a _____ in the sand.

Pam loves _____ and eggs.

Bob used a _____ on his trip.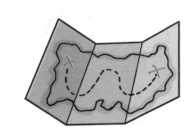

Add the letters in each box to make words from that word family. Write each word.

-an
f + an = _____
v + an = _____

-at
c + at = _____
h + at = _____

Use an -an or -at word from above to finish each sentence. The first one is done for you.

The ___van___ is blue.

The _____ is gray and white.

She wears a pink _____.

I have a _____ in my room.

Write -ell to finish each word.

b _____

w _____

sh _____

y _____

**Make more -ell words. Use the word wheel. Write the words.
The first one is done for you.**

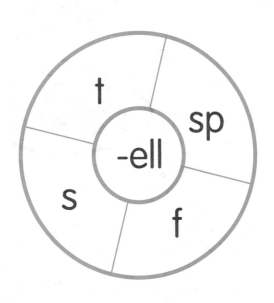

1. _____ spell _____

2. _____

3. _____

4. _____

Write -ick to finish each word.

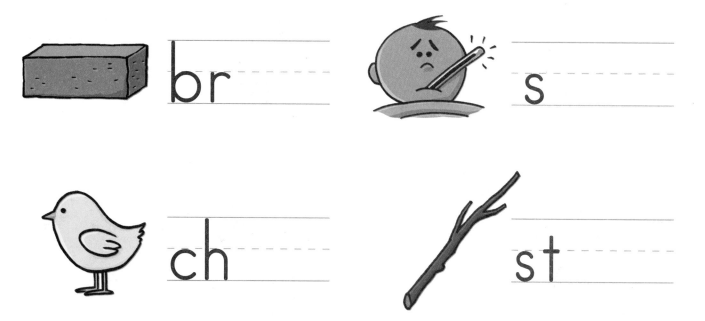

br _____

s _____

ch _____

st _____

Make more -ick words. Use the word wheel. Write the words. The first one is done for you.

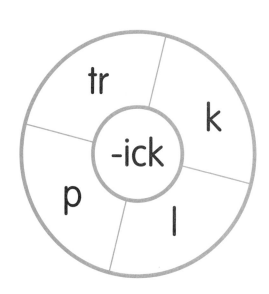

tr

k

-ick

p

l

1. _____ kick _____

2. _____

3. _____

4. _____

Write -ill to finish each word.

h

gr

dr

qu

Make more -ill words. Use the word wheel. Write the words. The first one is done for you.

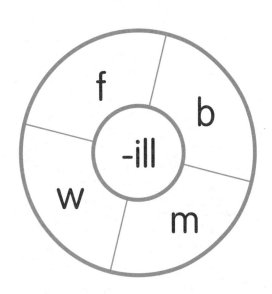

1. _____bill_____

2. _____

3. _____

4. _____

-ing

Write -ing to finish each word.

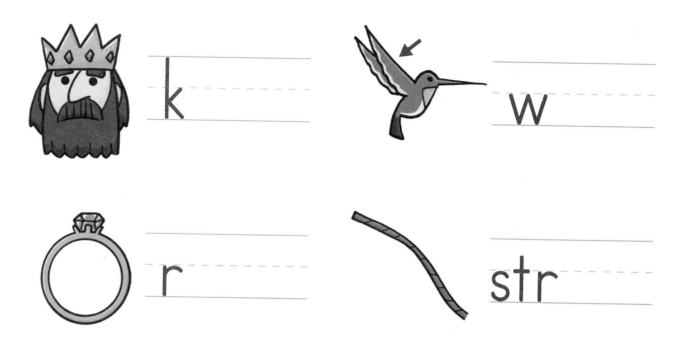

k _____

w _____

r _____

str _____

Make more -ing words. Use the word wheel. Write the words.
The first one is done for you.

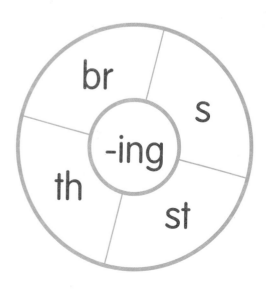

1. _____ sing _____

2. _____

3. _____

4. _____

Use the Letter Bank to complete the words in each row.

Letter Bank			
sm sh y	_____ell	_____ell	_____ell
br s st	_____ick	_____ick	_____ick
gr b sp	_____ill	_____ill	_____ill
w sw k	_____ing	_____ing	_____ing

Sort the words below into word families.
Write each word in the chart where it belongs.

ring   thick   sill   spring

brick   cell   quick   well

pick   will   sing   chill   wing

chick	shell	quill	king
1			
2			
3			
4			

How many of each did you find? Write the number below.

-ick ____   -ell ____   -ill ____   -ing ____

Which word family has the fewest words? _____

Add the letters in each box to make words in that word family. Write each word.

-ell	-ick
sh + ell = _____	k + ick = _____
b + ell = _____	st + ick = _____

Use an -ell or -ick word from above to finish each sentence. The first one is done for you.

The lunch ___bell___ rings at noon.

The dog brings the _____ back to me.

Dee found a pretty _____ on the shore.

Don't _____ the door.

Add the letters in each box to make words from that word family. Write each word.

-ill
gr + ill = _____
h + ill = _____

-ing
k + ing = _____
s + ing = _____

Use an -ill or -ing word from above to finish each sentence. The first one is done for you.

The house is just over that ___hill___.

My parents love to _____ in the summer.

The _____ lives in the castle.

Marci loves to _____.

19

Write -ip to finish each word.

dr _____

s _____

sh _____

tr _____

Make more -ip words. Use the word wheel. Write the words. The first one is done for you.

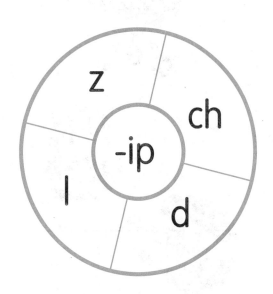

1. _____ chip _____

2. _____

3. _____

4. _____

Write -ock to finish each word.

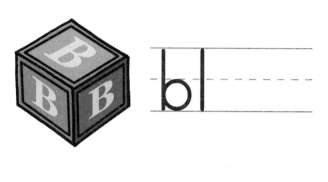 b|

 c|

 l

 s

Make more -ock words. Use the word wheel. Write the words.
The first one is done for you.

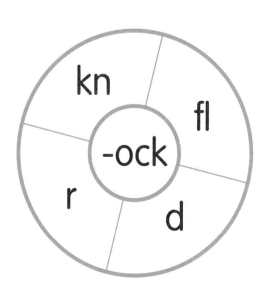

1. _____ flock _____

2. _____

3. _____

4. _____

© Scholastic Inc.

Write -op to finish each word.

m _____

s t _____

t _____

p _____

Make more -op words. Use the word wheel. Write the words. The first one is done for you.

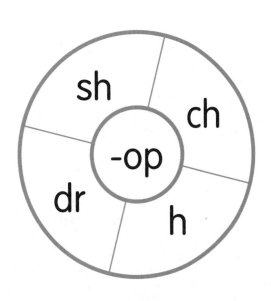

1. _____ chop _____

2. _____

3. _____

4. _____

Write -ug to finish each word.

b _____   r _____

j _____   s| _____

Make more -ug words. Use the word wheel. Write the words. The first one is done for you.

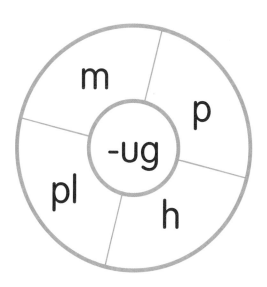

m

p

-ug

pl

h

1. _____ pug _____

2. _____

3. _____

4. _____

Use the Letter Bank to complete the words in each row.

Letter Bank			
sh s ch	_____ip	_____ip	_____ip
d r cl	_____ock	_____ock	_____ock
h st m	_____op	_____op	_____op
b m pl	_____ug	_____ug	_____ug

Sort the words below into word families.
Write each word in the chart where it belongs.

tip   knock   tug   drop

flop   zip   plug   mug

hug   lip   top   lock

ship	clock	stop	slug
1			
2			
3			
4			

How many of each did you find? Write the number below.

-ip _____   -ock_____   -op_____   -ug_____

Which two word families have the same number of words?

_____ and _____

Add the letters in each box to make words in that word family. Write each word.

-ip	-ock
sh + ip = _____	r + ock = _____
h + ip = _____	cl + ock = _____

Use an -ip or -ock word from above to finish each sentence. The first one is done for you.

Billy hurt his _____hip_____ playing hockey.

Zane sat on a _____.

The cruise _____ left this morning.

We need to repair the _____.

Add the letters in each box to make words from that word family. Write each word.

-op	-ug
m + op = _____	r + ug = _____
ch + op = _____	m + ug = _____

Use an -op or -ug word from above to finish each sentence. The first one is done for you.

We need a new ___rug___.

Let's _____ the floor.

This is my favorite _____.

Let's watch Dad _____ wood for the fire.

© Scholastic Inc.

-ail

Write -ail to finish each word.

m _____

p _____

qu _____

sn _____

Make more -ail words. Use the word wheel. Write the words.
The first one is done for you.

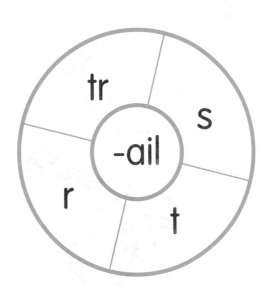

tr

s

-ail

r

t

1. _____ sail _____

2. _____

3. _____

4. _____

Write -ake to finish each word.

 c _____

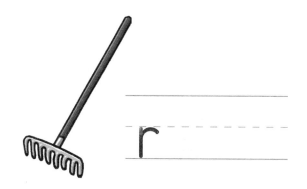 r _____

 l _____

 sn _____

Make more -ake words. Use the word wheel. Write the words. The first one is done for you.

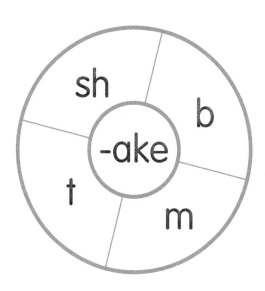

1. _____ bake _____

2. _____

3. _____

4. _____

-ay

Write **-ay** to finish each word.

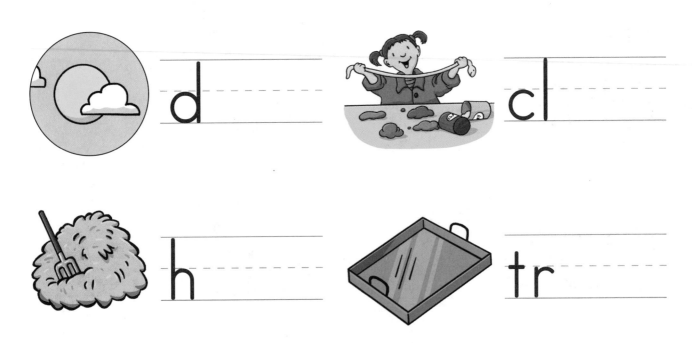

d _____

cl _____

h _____

tr _____

Make more **-ay** words. Use the word wheel. Write the words. The first one is done for you.

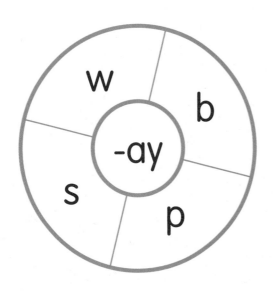

1. _____ bay _____

2. _____

3. _____

4. _____

Write -ee to finish each word.

b _____

thr _____

kn _____

tr _____

**Make more -ee words. Use the word wheel. Write the words.
The first one is done for you.**

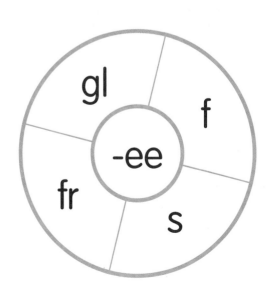

1. _____ fee _____

2. _____

3. _____

4. _____

Use the Letter Bank to complete the words in each row.

Letter Bank			
n s t	_____ail	_____ail	_____ail
w c r	_____ake	_____ake	_____ake
cl tr d	_____ay	_____ay	_____ay
b tr thr	_____ee	_____ee	_____ee

Sort the words below into word families.
Write each word in the chart where it belongs.

quake   gray   three   pail

sail   shake   tree

glee   stay   tail   trail

quail	cake	hay	bee
1			
2			
3			
4			

How many of each did you find? Write the number below.

-ail _____   -ake _____   -ay_____   -ee _____

Which word family has the most words? _____

**Add the letters in each box to make words in that word family.
Write each word.**

-ail	-ake
p + ail = _____	c + ake = _____
sn + ail = _____	l + ake = _____

**Use an -ail or -ake word from above to finish each sentence.
The first one is done for you.**

I saw a ___snail___ on the grass.

The _____ is frozen.

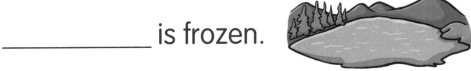

This _____ is good.

Noah has a red _____.

Add the letters in each box to make words from that word family. Write each word.

-ay
tr + ay = _____
h + ay = _____

-ee
tr + ee = _____
b + ee = _____

Use an -ay or -ee word from above to finish each sentence. The first one is done for you.

He was stung by a ___ bee ___.

Set the _____ on the table.

She likes to sit under the _____.

Horses eat _____.

© Scholastic Inc.

Write -eep to finish each word.

sh _____

sw _____

sl _____

st _____

Make more -eep words. Use the word wheel. Write the words. The first one is done for you.

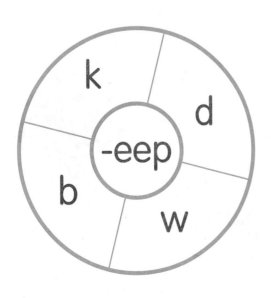

1. ___ deep ___

2. _____

3. _____

4. _____

Write -ice to finish each word.

 d _____

 s _____

 m _____

 r _____

Make more -ice words. Use the word wheel. Write the words.
The first one is done for you.

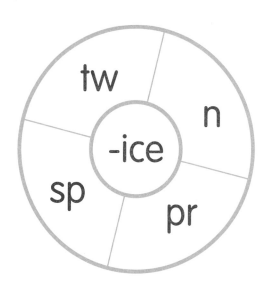

1. _____ nice _____

2. _____

3. _____

4. _____

-ight

Write **-ight** to finish each word.

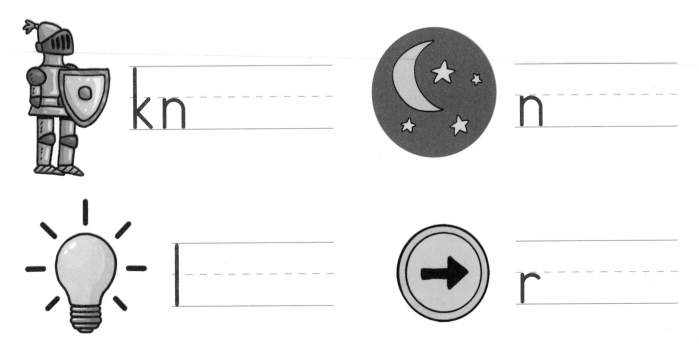

kn _ _ _ _ _ _ _ _

n _ _ _ _ _ _ _ _

l _ _ _ _ _ _ _ _

r _ _ _ _ _ _ _ _

Make more **-ight** words. Use the word wheel. Write the words. The first one is done for you.

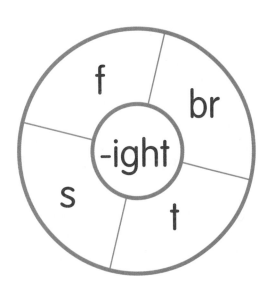

1. _____ bright _____

2. _____

3. _____

4. _____

Write -ow to finish each word.

b _____

sn _____

cr _____

bl _____

Make more -ow words. Use the word wheel. Write the words. The first one is done for you.

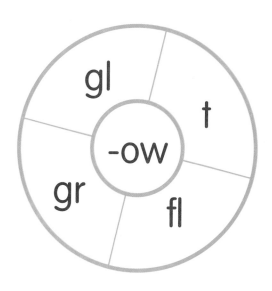

gl

t

-ow

gr

fl

1. _____ tow _____

2. _____

3. _____

4. _____

Use the Letter Bank to complete the words in each row.

Letter Bank			
st			
sw			
sh	_____eep	_____eep	_____eep
m			
sl			
r	_____ice	_____ice	_____ice
l			
r			
n	_____ight	_____ight	_____ight
b			
cr			
thr	_____ow	_____ow	_____ow

Sort the words below into word families.
Write each word in the chart where it belongs.

bright   price   grow   beep

deep   glow   mice   low

spice   tight   flow   keep

sheep	dice	right	bow
1			
2			
3			
4			

How many of each did you find? Write the number below.

-eep ____   -ice ____   -ight ____   -ow ____

Which word family has the fewest words? _____

Add the letters in each box to make words in that word family. Write each word.

-eep
sh + eep = _____
sl + eep = _____

-ice
d + ice = _____
r + ice = _____

Use an -eep or -ice word from above to finish each sentence. The first one is done for you.

Look at the pretty ___sheep___.

We need to _____ soon.

Roll the _____.

Jenny likes _____.

42

Add the letters in each box to make words from that word family.
Write each word.

-ight

l + ight = _____

n + ight = _____

-ow

sn + ow = _____

cr + ow = _____

Use an **-ight** or **-ow** word from above to finish each sentence.
The first one is done for you.

The ___light___ is very bright.

Stars come out at _____.

The _____ flew away.

Kate loves the _____.

Name each picture. Write the word.
Draw a line to match it to the correct word family.

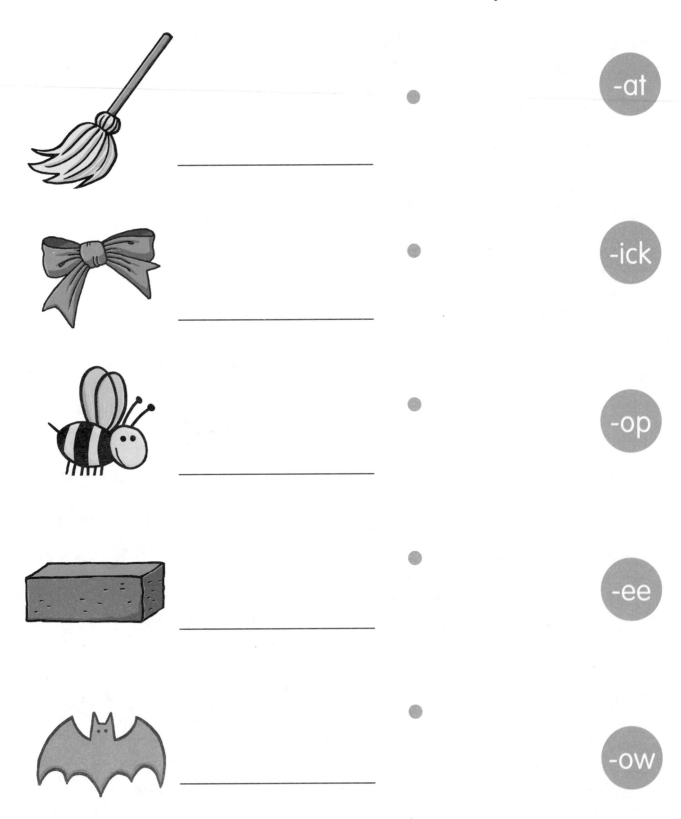

-at

-ick

-op

-ee

-ow

Name each picture. Write the word.
Draw a line to match it to the correct word family.

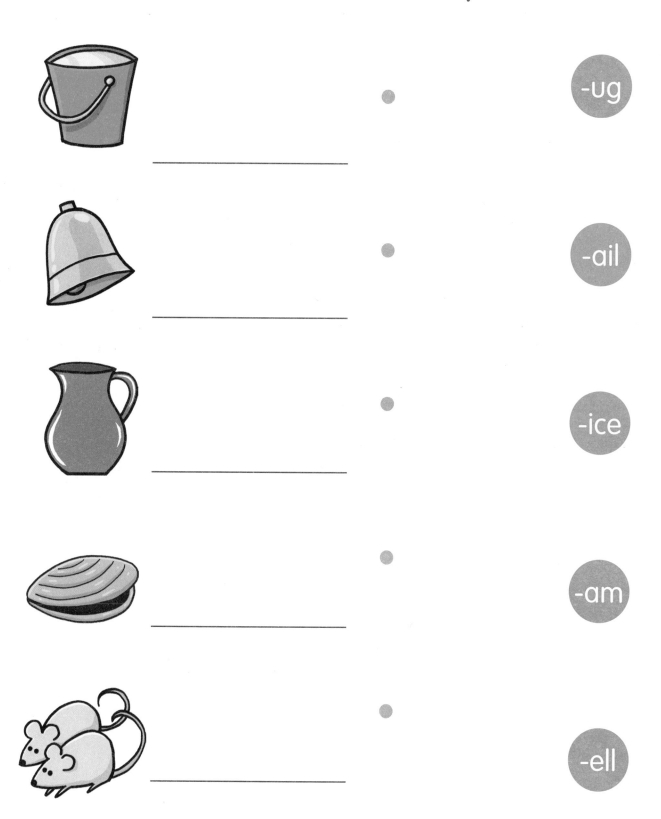

-ug

-ail

-ice

-am

-ell

Label each picture. Use the Word Box.
Match the pictures that are in the same word family.

Word Box					
clay	king	sheep	sweep	tray	ring

Label each picture. Use the Word Box.
Match the pictures that are in the same word family.

Word Box					
clap	clock	lock	map	ship	trip

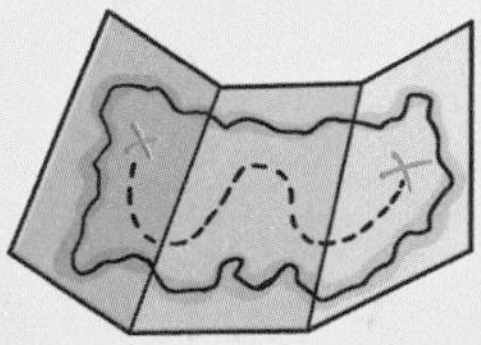

_____

_____

_____

_____

_____

_____

_____

Color the picture. Use the color key.

If the space has a word from this word family	-an	-ill	-ake	-eep	-ight
Color the space	blue	red	yellow	green	purple

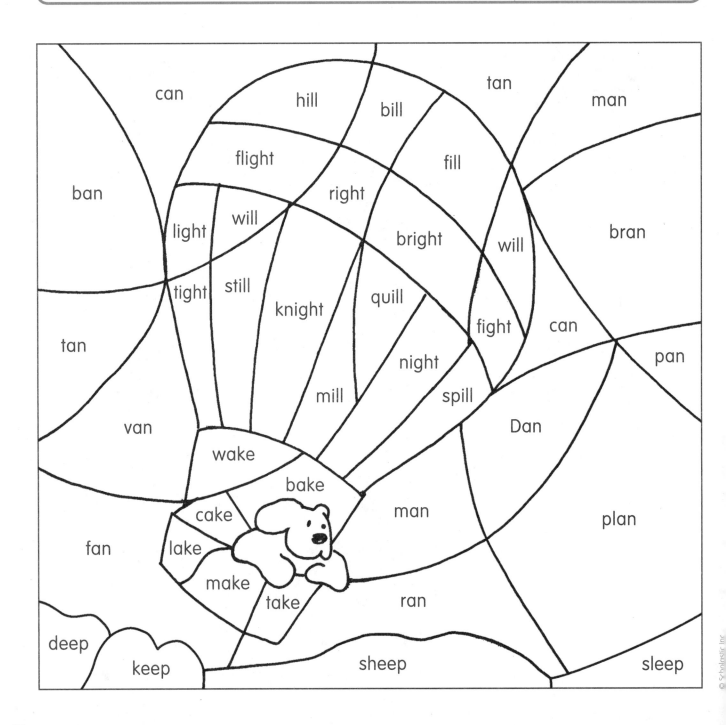